W9-AAF-988

Let's Play Tag!

📖 Read the Page

▶ Read the Story

🔄 Repeat

⏹ Stop

⭐ Game

💻

Chicka Chicka Boom Boom

by Bill Martin Jr
and
John Archambault

illustrated by
Lois Ehlert

A told **B**
and **B** told **C**,
"I'll meet you at the top
of the coconut tree."

"Whee!" said **D**
to **E F G**,
"I'll beat you to the top
of the coconut tree."

Chicka chicka boom boom!
Will there be enough room?
Here comes **H**
up the coconut tree,

and **I** and **J**
and tag–along **K**,
all on their way
up the coconut tree.

Chicka chicka boom boom!
Will there be enough room?
Look who's coming!
L M N O P!

m n o p

And Q R S!

And **T** **U** **V**!

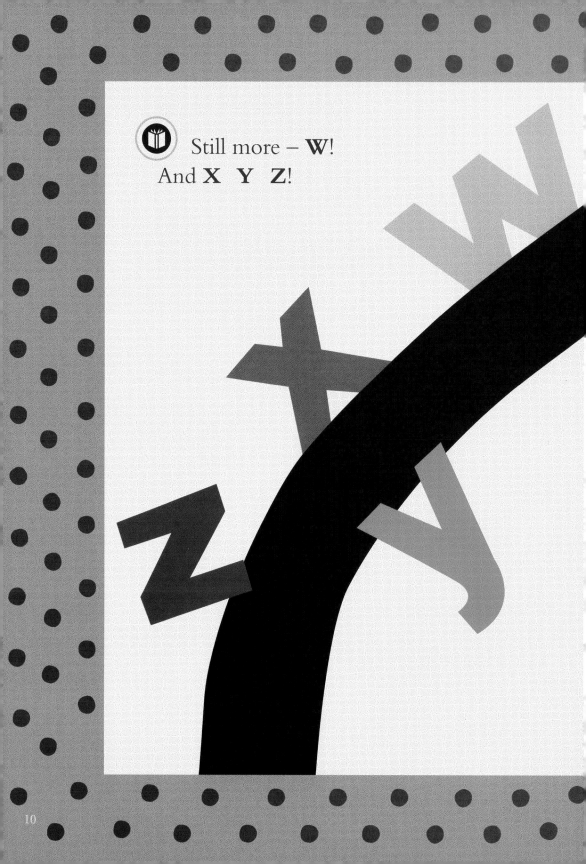

Still more – **W**!
And **X Y Z**!

The whole alphabet
up the – Oh, no!

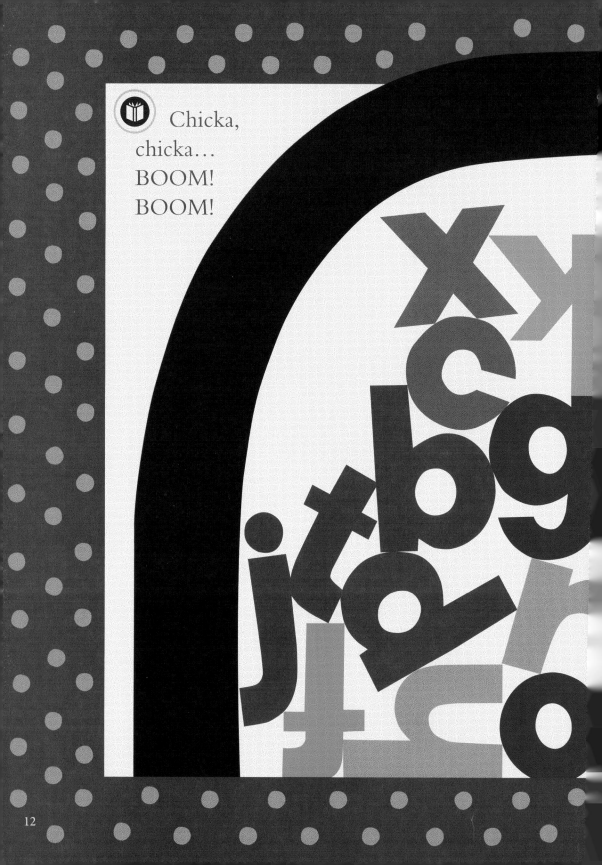

Chicka,
chicka…
BOOM!
BOOM!

Skit skat skoodle doot.
Flip flop flee.
Everybody running to the coconut tree.
Mamas and papas
and uncles and aunts
hug their little dears,
then dust their pants.

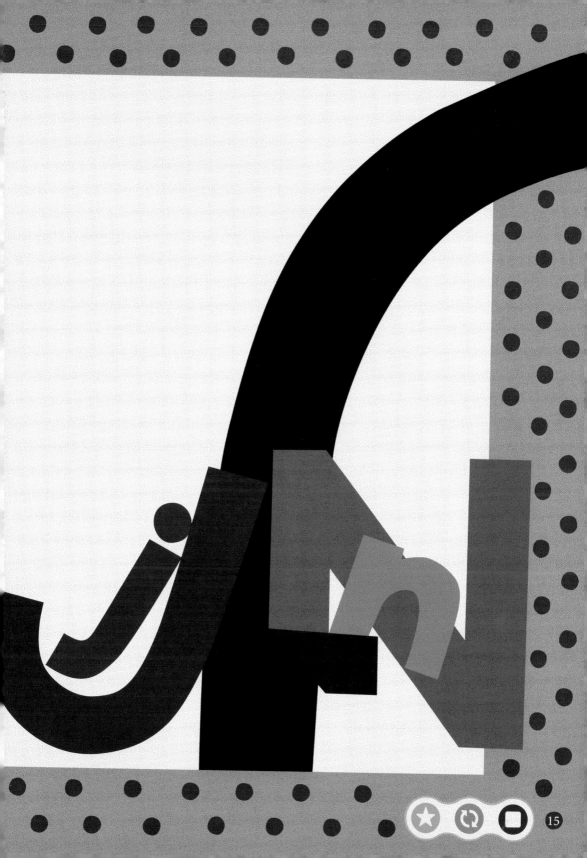

"Help us up," cried **A B C**.

Next from the pileup
skinned–knee **D**
and stubbed-toe **E**
and patched-up **F**.
Then comes **G**
all out of breath.

H is tangled up with **I**.
J and **K** are about to cry.
L is knotted like a tie.

M is looped.
N is stooped.
O is twisted alley-oop.
Skit skat skoodle doot.
Flip flop flee.

M is looped.
N is stooped.
O is twisted alley-oop.
Skit skat skoodle doot.
Flip flop flee.

Look who's coming!
It's black-eyed **P**,
Q R S,
and loose-tooth **T**.

pqrst

Look who's coming!
It's black-eyed **P**,
Q **R** **S**,
and loose-tooth **T**.

parst

Then **U V W**
wiggle-jiggle free.

Last to come
X Y Z.
And the sun goes down
on the coconut tree…

But —
chicka chicka boom boom!
Look, there's a full moon.

A is out of bed,
and this is what he said,
"Dare double dare,
you can't catch me.
I'll beat you to the top
of the coconut tree."
Chicka chicka
BOOM! BOOM!

AaBbC
FfGgH
LlMmN
QqRrS
VvWwX

cDdEe
hIiJjKk
nOoPp
sTtUu
xXyYyZz

33